BRITAIN IN OLD PHOTOGRAPHS

LYE & WOLLESCOTE

DENYS BROOKS &
PAT DUNN

SUTTON PUBLISHING LIMITED

Sutton Publishing Limited
Phoenix Mill · Thrupp · Stroud
Gloucestershire · GL5 2BU

First published 1997

Reprinted 1997

Copyright © Pat Dunn, 1997

British Library Cataloguing in Publication Data
A catalogue record for this book is available from the
British Library.

ISBN 0-7509-1657-5

Typeset in 10/12 Perpetua.
Typesetting and origination by
Sutton Publishing Limited.
Printed in Great Britain by
Ebenezer Baylis, Worcester.

THE BLACK COUNTRY SOCIETY

This voluntary society, affiliated to the Civic Trust, was founded
in 1967 as a reaction to the trend of the late 1950s and early 1960s
to amalgamate everything into large units and in the Midlands to
sweep away the area's industrial heritage in the process.

The general aim of the Society is to create interest in the past, present and future of
the Black Country, and early on it campaigned for the establishment of an industrial
museum. In 1975 the Black Country Museum was started by Dudley Borough Council
on 26 acres of totally derelict land adjoining the grounds of Dudley Castle. This has
developed into an award-winning museum which attracts over 250,000 visitors annually.

At the Black Country Museum there is a boat dock fully equipped to restore narrow
boats of wood and iron and different boats can be seen on the dock throughout the year.
From behind the Bottle and Glass Inn visitors can travel on a canal boat into Dudley
Canal Tunnel, a memorable journey to see spectacular limestone caverns and the
fascinating Castle Mill Basin.

There are over two thousand members of the Black Country Society and all receive
the quarterly magazine *The Blackcountryman*, of which over 119 issues have been
published since its founding in 1967. In the whole collection there are some 1,700
authoritative articles on all aspects of the Black Country by historians, teachers,
researchers, students, subject experts and ordinary folk with an extraordinary story to tell.
The whole constitutes a unique resource about the area and is a mine of information for
students and researchers who frequently refer to it. Many schools and libraries are
subscribers. Three thousand copies of the magazine are printed each quarter. It is non-
commercial, and contributors do not receive payment for their articles.

PO Box 71 · Kingswinford · West Midlands DY6 9YN

CONTENTS

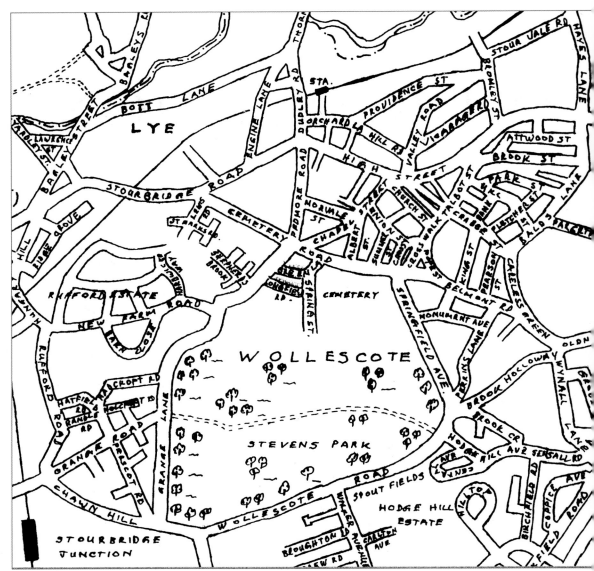

A sketch map of the area covered by the book; many of the streets completely disappeared in the widespread redevelopment of the 1960s.

INTRODUCTION

The three Black Country communities featured in this book all bear names of Saxon origin – Lye meaning pasture, Wollescote, Wulhere's cot, and Stambermill, stepping-stone brook mill. They were formerly in the ancient parish of Old Swinford and, before the reorganization of local government in the late nineteenth century, under the secular jurisdiction of Hales Owen.

Except for a brief period during the Civil War when Wollescote Hall was the local headquarters of Prince Rupert, life was uneventful, that is until the end of the seventeenth century when gypsies descended on the Waste, the uncultivated land beyond Lye proper which was centred around the Cross. Attracted by the area's prosperity and its raw materials, namely coal and fireclay, the newcomers built themselves crude mud houses – 103 being recorded on Waste Bank in 1699. As a result Lye is still often called Mud City. Although they settled and earned an uncertain living in the local trade of nail-making, the Lye Wasters failed to integrate with their Lye neighbours by whom they were regarded as a lawless and Godless lot.

In 1790 the Revd James Scott, a Unitarian Minister from Netherend, was the first to exercise a civilizing influence on the Waste, eventually building a permanent chapel there in 1806. In 1813 Thomas Hill, a local benefactor, was instrumental in the founding of an Anglican church fortuitously sited midway between the two settlements, thus encouraging their integration and bringing beneficial influences to bear on the Lye Wasters. It became the parish church in 1843. Wollescote was served by the Belmont Mission which was opened in 1878.

Various other religious groups were active locally in the nineteenth century, particularly the Methodists; a Wesleyan Chapel was erected in 1818, Primitive Methodist Chapel in 1831, Gospel Hall in 1884, Bethel Chapel in 1890 and Hayes Lane Chapel in 1896. A Congregational church was built in 1827. The Salvation Army also had an enormous impact when it appeared in 1881. All religious groups were zealous in providing opportunities for a basic education and the Non-Conformists in particular also offered their congregations experience in democratic organization, self-expression and self-help.

When the major occupation of nail-making by hand was ruined by foreign competition and mechanization, from the 1840s other industries developed. However, the invention of the frost cog by Henry Wooldridge of Lye in 1880 ensured that one facet of the trade survived. (A frost cog is a device fitted into a horseshoe to prevent the animal slipping in frosty or snowy weather.) The first local factory, built in 1770, was Thomas Perrins' chain works at Careless Green, but there were also small vice, anvil, spade and shovel works. The band of superior fireclay running from Wollescote to Kingswinford led to the manufacture of firebricks, furnace linings, crucibles for the glass industry and both plain and ornamental house bricks. Lye High Street still boasts fine edifices composed of the latter two products, particularly the Centre, Rhodes, and Bank Buildings.

However, it was the manufacture of hollow-ware which was to replace nail-making as the prime Lye industry. In the latter years of the nineteenth century buckets, baths, trunks and boxes were made. The labour force was cheap, plentiful and expert at handling metal. Technical advances, particularly galvanizing, introduced in 1863 by eighteen-year-old George Hill, led to further expansion and to Lye's other nickname, 'Bucket Capital of the World'. Vitreous enamelling was later to become as popular as galvanizing. However, in the twentieth century, plastics and other synthetics were to ruin this trade.

Factories introduced discipline, orderliness and a more secure income to the working population; there was also more time for leisure activities. In earlier days sports and pastimes had been bloodthirsty ones – bull- and badger-baiting, bare knuckle fighting and cock and dog fighting (though these latter two persisted illegally in Lye well into the present century). However, the influence of church and chapel introduced more civilized amusements: football and cricket teams, scout and guide troops, cultural classes, concerts and anniversary celebrations. Public houses had always abounded; in 1866 there were reputedly 53 pubs to serve a population of 7,000. These also began to field their own cricket and football teams, organize pigeon clubs, domino and dart matches, social trips and treats. In 1874 the Temperance Hall was built, followed by the Vic in 1913, both of which staged a variety of entertainments. The Clifton cinema opened in 1937. The annual carnivals in aid of the Corbett Hospital attracted tremendous support.

The entire community benefited greatly from the opening of a public park, the gift of local industrialist, Mr Ernest Stevens, who handed it over to the Lye and Wollescote Urban District Council in 1932. This body had been formed under new local government legislation in 1897; its members were forward-looking individuals who tackled slum clearance, introduced efficient sewerage disposal facilities and water supply to existing homes and built new council houses. Streets were improved by proper paving, lighting and cleaning. In 1933 the Council was disbanded when the area was incorporated into the Borough of Stourbridge.

Their involvement in church and chapel affairs encouraged Lye folk to enter local and national politics, to rise high in professions, to become inventors, artists, photographers, poets and actors. Many served the church, one became an archbishop, others ministers and missionaries. Two 'outsiders' who came to know the area immortalized Lye in literature – Annie S. Swan in her book *A Bitter Debt* and Sabine Baring-Gould in his *Nebo the Nailer*. Both provided vivid descriptions of the town in earlier days, a Lye barely recognizable after the massive redevelopment of the 1960s.

This volume has attempted to recapture glimpses of that Lye, including Wollescote and Stambermill. It is also a memorial to Denys Brooks, Lye's local historian, who collected many of the photographs and who died suddenly in January 1997 before this book was completed.

High Street at the turn of the century. This photograph shows the Bank Buildings on the right and the outbuildings of Alton House on the left. Note the lack of traffic compared with the congestion today.

STREET SCENES

Lye Cross, c. 1890, which shows the New Rose and Crown Inn, more popularly known as the 'Merica Bar because of the brass footrail around the counter. A 'hitching' rail also ran around the outside windows. In earlier times the area in front was the scene of fairs and such barbaric sports as bear- and bull-baiting. On the left can be seen the gables of the ancient Brocksopp's Hall.

This shot of the Upper High Street was taken before the 1960s redevelopment; on the left is Wassell's greengrocery store. Next door is the former Royal Oak, then 'Bill's Bakehouse'. Beyond is H. Case's ironmongery shop on the far corner of Pump Street.

Upper High Street again. On the second building on the left is the barber's pole of George Russell's salon. The tower belongs to the Unitarian Church erected in 1861 on the site of the Revd James Scott's original chapel of 1806; the clock commemorated his life and work. It was replaced in 1953 with an illuminated model to celebrate Queen Elizabeth's coronation. Note the overhead tram cables.

The High Street between Love Lane and Chapel Street. Taken immediately before redevelopment it shows, nearest the camera, Slater and Hughes' furniture store and Pharaoh Adams' butcher's shop. Beyond is a coach parked beside Collins' fruiterer's shop. Lying back is the Old Bell public house and on the corner is the old bank.

The same area under snow in 1962. There are signs of redevelopment in Love Lane where the Christmas tree is standing. The Clifton cinema lies back from the street, to the right of the three shops.

A view of the High Street from Chapel Street junction, *c.* 1910. The tram is *en route* to the terminus at the Hayes. The large house on the left, Alton House, was the home of the Mobberley family, prominent local brick manufacturers. It later served as the first library and council house.

The dedication of the war memorial, 23 October 1926. It was unveiled outside the parish church by Brigadier-General O.D. Hickman (holding the top hat). To the left of the Union Jack, supported by a crutch, is Mr Douglas Pielou, Conservative MP for Stourbridge, accompanied by his wife.

The opening of the new public library by Cedric Hardwicke, May 1935. It was built on the site of Alton House on the corner of Chapel Street and High Street. The Bank Buildings can be seen on the opposite side of the High Street.

Johnny Webb, a well-known Lye character in the late 1960s. He was a 'tatter' (rag and bone man) by trade and although he had an artificial leg was often seen riding a bicycle. The Spar shop behind him was built on the site of the Vic theatre.

Lye High Street looking towards the church from the Cross, *c.* 1902. Robins' grocery shop is in the left foreground and next to the hut is the 'Stute, the Working Men's Institute. The fine Rhodes buildings are top left. Note the cobbled street and the tram lines allowing vehicles to cross.

A tram traversing Lye Cross, *c.* 1902. On the left is Harvey's barber's and tobacconist's shop, the Centre buildings are opposite, while the second shop window on the right is that of the fabulous 'Ye Olde Antique Shoppe', featured in Annie S. Swan's book, *A Bitter Debt*.

Lye Cross in the 1950s. The 'Merica Bar is on the left corner and Harvey's barber's shop is opposite. Featureless modern shops have replaced Webster's antique shop, but the Institute remains.

Lye Cross, c. 1900. Harvey's barber's shop is on the left and opposite left are Elisha Cartwright's tailoring factory and the eighteenth-century 'Gothic' façade of Lye Cross House, birthplace of Cedric Hardwicke.

Love Lane, early 1960s. Postman Phillip Wooldridge is on his rounds. The factory on the right is Ray Westwood's joinery works. The Primitive Methodist Chapel is opposite, out of sight.

Looking up Church Street before redevelopment. The building with steps and 'deck' on the far right had once been the nail warehouse of Sargeant Turner before he converted to the hollow-ware trade. The scrolled sign belongs to the Liberal Club, opened on 30 July 1906.

The view from the top of Church Street, 1960s. 'Johnty' Perks' factory is on the left. It had started as a nail and frost cog concern, but diversified with the decline of the nail trade.

Another 1960s view of Church Street. Note the backstreet shop with its advertising signs on the left. The parish church spire is visible at the bottom of the hill.

Chapel Street before redevelopment. On the right beyond the car is the former police station. The three-storey building was the sleeping quarters for unmarried policemen.

A view of the Dock before it fell victim to redevelopment. It has been suggested that its name came from the practice of docking young horses' tails there. On the right is Jeavons' bungalow bath works. A bungalow bath was one that was not plumbed in. It was very popular in places like India as it could be put away after use.

An Edwardian postcard of Hill Road. It was named after Thomas Hill who built Lye church in 1813. The original vicarage can just be seen through the trees on the left. Some of the houses on the right still survive, as does the Orchard Lane School caretaker's house built at a right angle to them.

A 1960s view of Dudley Road, looking towards the Thorns. The shop on the right was Fletcher's the grocers. Lower down on the same side is the site of Lye Forge, founded in 1699, which made swords, armour and farm implements using the power of the River Stour. Its founders, the Folkes family, are still local industrialists.

Another 1960s view of Dudley Road. This photograph was taken from the Cross. Heathcock's coal office is on the right and the wall on the left is the garden wall of Lye Cross House.

Pedmore Road, mid-1920s. The terrace beyond the telephone pole on the left included the telephone exchange (number 16). It was opened on Tuesday 20 May 1890 with three numbers. It also served Stourbridge and Cradley Heath for a time.

A view looking towards the Grange, *c.* 1960. The house on the right with its window projecting into Pedmore Road was always known as the Toll House and indeed the road would have been a turnpike road in earlier days.

A view of the junction of Pedmore Road and Shepherd's Brook Road, *c.* 1960. The Toll House is at the top right-hand corner of the picture, recognizable by its two chimney pots.

A ship's figurehead which stood in a garden in Stourbridge Road for over fifty years. It was reputed to be from the Royal George which was launched in 1827 and broken up in 1875. It portrays George IV as a Roman emperor. It was originally one of Mr Henry Wooldridge's curios.

A typical backstreet shop before redevelopment. Note the YZ chewing gum dispenser and wealth of advertisements. Also featured is the Vine Inn. This is Union Street where William Booth, founder of the Salvation Army, was accommodated in 1863 when he conducted a six-week mission in Lye, prior to founding the Salvation Army. His wife, Catherine, was much taken with Lye folk.

Lye Waste with Brook Street and Pump Street on the left and right. This is a view looking up Talbot Street. Baker's clothing shop is on the right. This photograph was taken at the outset of the 1960s redevelopment of the area.

Corn Walks during the first stage of the Lye redevelopment plan. The bay-windowed building on the right is the Webb and Bashford warehouse. The shop with the 'ornate' frontage next to it belonged to Stan Bedford, a well-known 'hawker' and former frost cog manufacturer.

Skelding's Lane at its junction with Fanny's Lane; it ran straight down to the High Street. There are two public houses in view, on the right the Hundred House and the Lord Dudley Arms in the centre. Many years ago the area on the left was known as the Slack Mound; this view, however, dates from the 1960s.

A 1960s view of Cross Street as it joins Cross Walks. The well-known Darby's fish, fruit and vegetable shop is in the centre background on Cross Walks.

A mud hut in Skeldings Lane, *c.* 1910. It is reputed to be the original Hundred House pub. Note the thatched roof, the brick casing on the mud and the fly-posters. Two of the women wear men's caps, then a common sight, but a custom in vogue with a few older ladies even in the 1960s.

A pre-redevelopment view of Pope Street; it was named after a Lye family of that name. This photograph shows it at its junction with Belmont Road. On the far right is the driveway to the Top Bell public house.

Looking down Pope Street from the Top Bell, this photograph illustrates the Lye practice of throwing up houses without any pretence of planning. The wall on the right belongs to the Bell. Note the church spire and factory chimney in the distance, and the lack of pavements in the street.

Mr Ernest Stevens, the local industrialist and public benefactor, cutting the tape at the opening of Springfield Avenue in July 1931. At his left is George Henry Eveson and to his right is James Albert Gauden with other members of Lye and Wollescote Urban District Council. Behind the crowd are Ludgebridge Brook cottages.

A view of early twentieth-century Perrins Lane. The terrace would have been modern then. Monument Avenue on the left has no vehicular access into the lane because of the strategically placed tree stump. Note the absence of a footpath, or indeed, a decent road surface.

An earlier view of Perrins Lane. The only buildings are a scattering of cottages and chain shops, possibly the site of the original Perrins' chain works.

Another view of Perrins Lane in its early days. Note the chain shops and also the shutters on the cottage windows. The road has no pavement and a poor surface but does have a street lamp.

A view of Perrins Lane from the other direction. The house on the right with its chapel-like porch still stands, although now covered with plaster. The adjoining chain shop has disappeared. The cottages and chain shops beyond, on the left, are those in the previous two photographs.

A rustic Wollescote scene, *c.* 1900. Presumably 'Old Noll' is the bank on the left. The lane beside it wends its way to a row of cottages and the brook at the bottom. Today Stevens Park, Wollescote, is on the left and the lane is now called Wollescote Road.

Another rural Wollescote view showing Ludgebridge Brook cottages. They stood at the bottom of Perrins Lane and would appear to be farm labourers' cottages. In the 1851 census, however, every tenant was listed as a nail-maker, but there were three farms within a quarter of a mile of them in the early 1930s.

Another view of Ludgebridge Brook and the picturesque cottages. In this photograph there are no other buildings in sight; nowadays the cottages have gone, the land in the background is covered with houses and there is a large 1930s council estate to the right and Lye Park is on the left.

A waterfall on Ludgebridge Brook. This was in the Dingle which bordered a footpath between the council houses on Wollescote Road and the park playing fields. The brook later becomes Shepherd's Brook, flowing on through Stambermill and joining the Stour at Bagley Street. The power of the River Stour was used to drive mills and forges.

BUILDINGS

An early picture of Elisha Cartwright's clothing shop in Stourbridge Road. It was known as the Centre Building, the name at the top being the first outdoor electric illumination in Lye. Mr Cartwright named his son Centre. At the rear is the tailoring workshop often referred to as 'the chapel' which he built in 1897, possibly on the site of a chapel associated with Lye Cross House many years before.

Brocksopp's Hall in Dudley Road. This house pre-dated the Civil War and boasted a priest's hole. In the
First World War it was a haven for Belgian refugees but was gutted by fire in 1938. The corn stores on the
left belonged to the Evans's, an old Lye family.

Wollescote Hall, a seventeenth-century house built on the site of an earlier house. It was once the home of
the wealthy Milward family and during the Civil War was briefly the local headquarters of Prince Rupert.
It was purchased by Mr Ernest Stevens, together with its extensive grounds, and he presented them to Lye
and Wollescote UDC as a public park in 1932.

Lye Cross House, a late Stuart building, fronting the High Street and Dudley Road. It was the parental home and birthplace of Cedric Hardwicke, the celebrated actor, whose father was the local doctor. Although many individuals, including Adrian Hill, son of a local optician, made great efforts to save it, it fell victim to redevelopment on 20 June 1967.

Hay Green House. This was later the home of Mr Harry Morgan, partner in the well-known firm of builders' merchants, Morgan and Chance. Here it is decorated for King George V's Jubilee in 1936.

The building on the corner of Connop's Lane. Although somewhat dilapidated in this 1960s photograph, in its heyday it must have been a house of some importance. For several years it was a branch of Hill and Reading, a well-known firm of grocers.

A mud hut awaiting demolition in the 1960s. Such houses, built in large numbers on Lye Waste, earned the town the nickname of Mud City. Notice the brickwork replacing part of the mud walls.

The last mud hut in Lye. Situated on Cross Walks, it was demolished in the 1960s. Many houses in that area were early DIY efforts: walls were of local clay mixed with straw, roofs were often thatched.

The demolition of a mud hut. This photograph once more illustrates how brickwork often replaced clay in such houses. Although the original structures appeared very crude they were strong and long-lasting; so-called improvements reduced these qualities.

Army Row. Few families or places in Lye escaped having a nickname, and this terrace in Church Street was no exception. It was so called because of its proximity to the Salvation Army Citadel.

Three important buildings in Church Street. On the left is the Temperance Hall, designed by J.M. Gething and built in 1874. In its early years it served as concert hall, political forum, evangelical centre and playhouse. After 1910 it was a cinema seating 460 people. The gaping hole next to it was the first fire station (a handcart manned by volunteers) and the end building was the old police station.

The destruction of the Temp during the 1960s redevelopment. It had closed down in 1956 but reopened the following year. The projectionist's box can be seen on the left at the top.

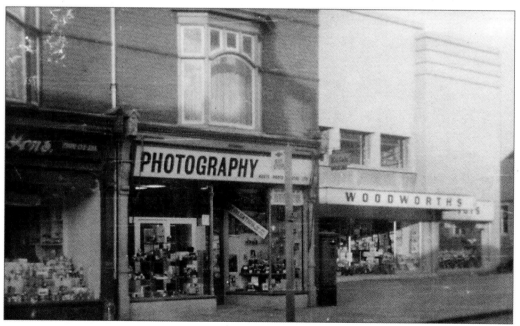

Three shops at the top of the High Street. On the left is Harry Barlow and Sons, grocer's, and Bill Hart's photography shop is next door. Last was the former Clifton cinema, built in 1937 to seat 1,100 people. Falling attendances led to its closure and the premises were taken over by Woodworths of Stourbridge, specialist toy retailers. It is now the town market.

The Old Bell or Bottom Bell. It stood in the High Street and for many years the landlord was Mr David Millward, contemporary and cricketing companion of Cedric Hardwicke. On the right is the old bank and on the left the former premises of Mr Albert Collins' greengrocery shop; he was also proprietor of the Favourite Coaches, a small motor-coach firm.

The old bank on the corner of High Street and Chapel Street. On the opposite corner was the library. In its life the bank building also served as UDC offices, a solicitor's office and a doctor's and dentist's surgery.

The original Working Men's Institute, popularly known as the 'Stute, built in 1856. In 1874 it was the scene of serious rioting during the Parliamentary elections. In about 1901 it underwent considerable alterations and continued to function until 1960. Lloyds Bank now occupies the site.

A gathering outside the 'Stute to celebrate the Coronation of Edward VII in 1902. Note the cobbled street and the tram lines in the foreground.

No. 175 High Street. This was the parental home of William (Bill) Pardoe; it was situated opposite the church and to the right of the Co-op. Both sites are now occupied by Barclays Bank. Mr Pardoe senior was a photographer like his son and this photograph was probably taken by him during the First World War.

Lye post office, c. 1910. It is the building on the right with the sign and was managed by the Freeman family; their daughter Dorothy was a noted singer and often appeared with Cedric Hardwicke in his youthful dramatic exploits. Next door was Butler's butcher's shop; its outbuildings were the original headquarters of the Lye branch of Toc H.

Ye Olde Antique Shoppe in the High Street. Mr Webster, the proprietor, was involved in a lengthy battle with the local council who accused him of advertising his business on his wife's gravestone and removed it from the churchyard. Mr Webster put it back – and so it went on until the matter was resolved in 1898 by the Bishop of Worcester. He said that the church and not the council had jurisdiction in the matter and supported Mr Webster.

Robins' grocery shop. This was in the High Street just past the Institute and was captured on film at the beginning of the century. Note the boy's Eton collar and the little girl's hat.

J.T. Worton's draper's shop. This was in the High Street next to the Congregational church, more commonly known as Woods Chapel. Mr Worton, who lived over the shop, was a prominent member of the Primitive Methodist Chapel and for many years represented Lye on Worcestershire County Council.

Meshak Lavender's tailor's shop. Although situated in the high street of working-class, industrial Lye, this old established business specialized in hunting pinks, jodhpurs and hacking jackets for the local gentry and hunting fraternity. In the 1874 elections, when serious disturbances broke out, the militia was despatched and the Riot Act was read from the shop doorway, reputedly for the last time anywhere in the country.

Weston's Shop, Stourbridge Road. The Westons were an old (and large) Lye family who traded in Hay Green for many years. This shop was housed in premises which had once been the Lamb Inn. This photograph shows Mr George and Mrs Sarah Weston and their daughter.

The drapery emporium, Love Lane. Mrs Obedience Dickens stands outside her shop which had originally been the first Co-operative store to open in Lye or indeed anywhere in the Birmingham area. It disappeared in the 1960s redevelopment.

Kitson's Stores, Cross Walks, *c.* 1900. Mrs Kitson stands proudly outside her grocery shop watched by an interested group of bystanders. The passageway on the left is one of the alleys of the Waste Bank. To the right is Pope Street. Note the enamelled signs advertising Venus soap and also the shutters on the windows, once a common feature of Lye houses.

The former Stambermill post office, 1920s. Mr and Mrs Johnson kept the premises and Mrs Johnson, widowed young, carried on alone for many years. This photograph shows their sons, Leslie and Fred, standing in the doorway. Until it closed some years ago the same sign was used over the succeeding post office on the corner of Bagley Street. The Johnson premises are now occupied by Clifford Hill.

Weston's shop, 176 Stourbridge Road, 1950s. This building still stands. Here, daughter Anne is in the doorway. The back garden overlooked the cricket ground and Mrs Weston supplied teas to the players for several years.

Morris, the jewellers, Stourbridge Road. Mr Morris, who is standing on the left, was a prominent member of St Mark's Church, Stambermill. His son, Edwin (first right), became Archbishop of Wales. This picture was taken at the turn of the century.

Noah's Ark Inn. This stood nearer to Lye Cross and on the opposite side of the road to the present one. For many years the licensee was Harry Holmes, a popular druggist in Lye High Street.

The Old Pear Tree on The Hayes. Mr Joseph Nock and son pose outside. The building still stands next to Brown's scrapyard. Note the slot machine and bus timetable on the right.

The Holly Bush, Cemetery Road. This was an old-established public house. In the doorway stands the landlord, George Henry Bromley, whose family kept a paint store in the High Street for many years. The pub owner was Jack Penn whose brewery was in Cross Walks Road at the Queen's Head.

The Crown Inn, Dudley Road. This was one of six public houses which flourished on that road. On the right stands the landlady, Mrs Joseph Kendrick, with her daughters Sadie, in the window, and Alice, in the doorway. The younger girls are twins Rose and Elsie Collins with their nephew Raymond.

Lye GWR station seen from Dudley Road bridge and looking towards Birmingham. The stairway on the left was for the sole use of Orchard House, the building covered with ivy. The long driveway of this house, built by local brick manufacturer, George King Harrison, extended into Orchard Lane but disappeared with the opening of the Stourbridge–Cradley Heath railway in 1863.

A view of Lye GWR station, taken from the footbridge and looking towards Stourbridge and the Dudley Road bridge. Engine no. 5185 is approaching with the 10.14 train to Birmingham Snow Hill on 1 June 1957. Orchard House is on the right. It still stands today, a wonderful testimony to Lye bricks.

Hungary Hill, Stambermill, showing between-the-wars private houses. Council houses were built opposite a little later. This is the area reputedly populated by Huguenot refugees from the continent in the seventeenth century, who brought their secrets of glass-making with them.

A unique view of the parish church and parsonage when all the land beyond, as far as Vicarage Road, was open ground. The church was built with bricks made on site in 1813 as a chapel of ease to Oldswinford church, mainly through the generosity of Thomas Hill. It became the parish church in 1843. The spire, designed by Owen Freeman, was added in 1885.

CHAPELS & CHURCHES

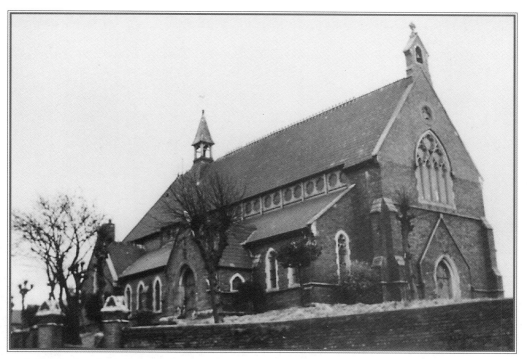

St Mark's, Stambermill. Opened in 1870 by Lord Lyttelton it was a sister to Lye parish church, services having been held in the local church school for several years previously. Always evangelical, it was in the patronage of the Church Pastoral Aid Society.

A bible class, St Mark's, *c.* 1930. The class leader was layman Edward Allport, seated in the midst of the ladies in the second row. He owned a draper's shop in Lye High Street and was a member of Lye and Wollescote Urban District Council.

A St Mark's choir outing to Ludlow. In the centre is the vicar, Revd A.G. Lewis, who served the parish for almost forty years. Seated on his left is Mr Alfred Morris (father of Archbishop Morris) whose marriage to Maria Beatrice Lickert was reputedly the first to be solemnized at St Mark's.

St Mark's centenary celebrations, December 1970. The Vicar, Revd H. Winterburn, wardens J. Chance and E. Hazeldine and choir are photographed with the recently retired Archbishop of Wales, Rt Revd A.E. Morris, MA, DD.

Lye parish church, an early photograph taken before the addition of the spire in 1885. Its official title is Christ Church and it opened for worship on 5 December 1813 with its first perpetual curate, Matthew Booker, in charge.

Revd James Bromley, vicar of Lye, 1845–65.
He was a much loved pastor and when he died
suddenly a public appeal raised £3,000 for his
large family when the living was only worth
£240 per annum. He is reputed to have loved
flowers and in this photograph holds a rose.

Lye church choir in 1917. The Revd J.T. Conan-Davies is seated in the middle row. The short man in the
centre of the back row is Arthur Taylor, the organist. Is it possible that the young man on his left had
forgotten his surplice and was made to hide?

Lye church choir in 1930. The Revd C.M. Stuart-King poses with the choir outside the church porch. In the centre, at the rear, is Clarence Chance, the organist and nephew of Mr Arthur Taylor who held the same position in the 1917 photograph.

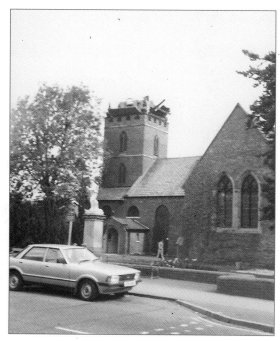

Lye church minus its spire. Christ Church underwent major alterations in the mid-1980s and among them was the removal of the spire which had become unsafe. This photograph shows the operation almost complete.

Belmont Mission. A chapel of ease to Lye church, it was situated on Waste Bank, now Hill Bank. Built in 1878 it replaced a wooden structure and served the area well until the opening of St Andrew's, Wollescote, in 1939. It was then sold and this photograph shows it in use as a factory. The bell was later installed at St Andrew's.

Belmont Sunday school teachers, 1935. Back row, left to right: Percy Mallen, Gilbert Taylor, Meg Hodges, Harry Hart, Ethel Cartwright, Leslie Pearson. Front row: Mrs Hodges, Edith Darby, Vera Darby, Mr Hodges, Alice Davies, Marie Westwood, Mrs Allen. The toddler is Margaret Hill.

A break for refreshment on the Belmont Ramble – some young people from Belmont Mission. They are, left to right, Leslie Pearson, Beatrice Wassell, ? Skidmore, Henry Hart, Alice Smith, Betty Hodges, Walter Taylor, Bill Hodges. Judging by the youth of Leslie and Henry this picture pre-dates the previous photograph.

A view of Mount Tabor Chapel on Lye Waste. In true Lye fashion it was always known as 'Top Chapel'. It was opened in 1872 and closed in 1964 when its congregation moved to St John's.

A view of the east end of Mount Tabor Chapel before its demolition during the 1960s redevelopment of the Waste.

The Unitarian parsonage was situated close to the Top Bell public house in Belmont Road. Pictured are the Wrigley family. The Revd Mr Wrigley was a well-respected individual, a local councillor and tireless champion of good causes during his ministry in Lye which lasted from 1891 to 1924. His wife was a qualified teacher.

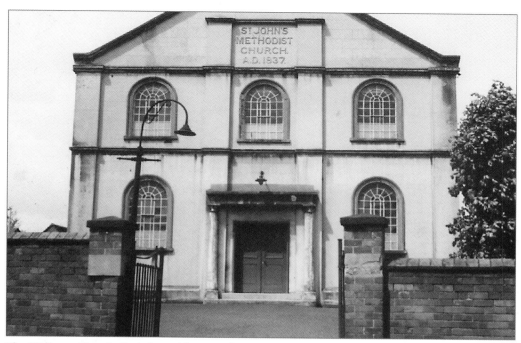

The Wesleyan Chapel, Dark Lane. This was afterwards known as St John's Methodist Church in Chapel Street. It was built on the site of the earlier chapel in 1837 and was closed in 1968. Its congregation now forms part of that of the United Church in the High Street.

St John's autumn fair. This mid-1960s photograph records the opening of the fair by Wolves and England International footballer, Roy Swinbourne. Local businessman Alan Thompson, chairman of the fund-raising committee, is on the left and the minister, Revd Amos Edwards, is on the right.

Stambermill Congregational Chapel, *c.* 1914. Originally built as a New Connexion Methodist Church in 1839 it became a Congregational Church in 1894. It produced an enormous number of missionaries, including John Robinson, one of the first ever to be sent to China.

A Congregational speakers' class. This early twentieth-century group includes Mr W.G. Harbach, for many years a brush manufacturer with premises in Union Passage. He is in the centre of the back row.

Congregational Sunday school teachers pose outside the manse. Mr Harbach is among them, sitting in the centre of the middle row. Note the large, fashionable hats of the ladies which suggest a date of about 1910.

The end of the Prims (Primitive Methodist church), July 1974. Largely as a result of building work taking place around the church in Love Lane, part of the structure collapsed. This picture shows a gaping hole where the organ had been. In the year that the tabernacle opened after rebuilding, in 1863, the Prims played host to William Booth, later to found the Salvation Army. He conducted a six-week mission in Lye.

Leaders' class, the Prims. The leaders were lay people who led adult classes in Bible studies and other topics. Always a strong well-supported church, this old photograph shows a class of twenty-seven men. Second from the right on the second row is a young Mr J. T. Worton, JP, local draper and loyal member of the church throughout his life.

Prims' teachers, c. 1928. A much older Mr Worton, seated beside his wife, is in the second row, fourth from the left.

Prim's Sunday school, Connop's Lane. This is a building unique in political history for here, in May 1918, before women had the vote, the first woman to be adopted to contest a Parliamentary seat was nominated at a meeting. She was Mary MacArthur who had sometime previously led the women chain-makers at Cradley Heath in their struggle for better wages and conditions.

A wartime Salem Chapel group. Salem Chapel in Pedmore Road was built in 1893. Mr G. King Harrison, a local brick manufacturer, donated 10,000 white bricks and other businessmen gave building materials and furnishings. Designed by Owen Freeman, it cost £450 to build. In this photograph are, front row, left to right, ? Gardener, Arthur Porter, Betty Gardener, Charles Dickens, ? Gardener, Len Southall, Ray Perks. Back row: Joe Cooper, Edgar Perks, Arthur Gardener, Walter Hazelwood, Ken Pearson, Len Perks.

Hayes Lane Methodist Chapel Sunday school teachers, 1933. The chapel was built in 1896. Featured in this photograph are, back row, left to right, Charles Hill, Harold Johnson. Front row: Doris Johnson, Lily Pearson, Margaret Hill, Irene Hall, Gladys Hough, Mrs J. Willetts. The boy is Norman Hough.

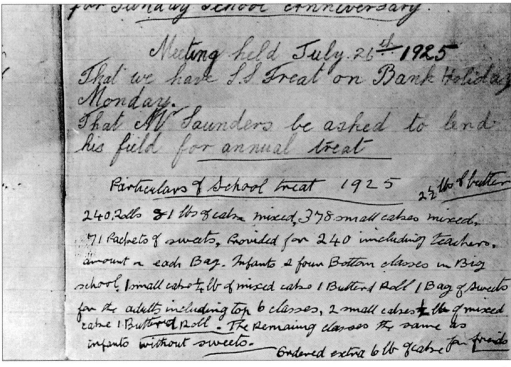

An extract from Hayes Lane minute book, 1925. It gives details of the Sunday school treat, a simple pleasure, but for many the highlight of the year.

'The Junior Workers of Bucket Town.' This photograph appeared in the Salvation Army magazine, the *Young Soldier*, in January 1913. Standing, left to right, are cadets Ettie Gordon, Mary Brettell, Alice Cartwright, Rosanna Brettell, Annie Halford, May Brettell, Mrs Hart, Martha Chapman, Jessie Boulter. Seated are M. Chapman, Mrs Dewey, Sergeant-Major A. Green, Mrs Winmill, Captain Bowen, Mrs Munn, Florrie Phillips.

The Salvation Army band, probably photographed at the presentation of new instruments. The shot was taken in the field where, in 1937, the Clifton cinema was built. Behind are two houses in Hill Road, built and occupied by brothers John and David Croft, hollow-ware manufacturers at Wollescote.

The anniversary of the Salvation Army, this picture shows the decorated platform in the Church Street Citadel. On the left of the front row is Alfred Rose, the local doctor and a frequent and popular speaker at Army functions.

J.V. Kendrick was a familiar figure in all the churches and chapels and was probably more well known in the homes of Lye than any other individual. He was the local undertaker and is pictured here with his 1966 Rolls-Royce.

SCHOOLS

Orchard Lane School, which opened in 1882. It was previously accommodated in the rented premises of the Congregational Chapel in order to comply with the 1870 Education Act, requiring all children to have access to education. The new school had three departments, mixed infants, boys and girls. It was administered by a locally elected, voluntary School Board which met in a room under the bell turret. This photograph was taken within a short time of its opening.

Adult morning class, Stambermill Congregational Chapel, 1912. This photograph illustrates the fact that, before the state was active in education, churches and chapels had from their earliest beginnings striven to educate both young and old. This class met at 8 a.m. on a Sunday morning and studied both secular and religious subjects.

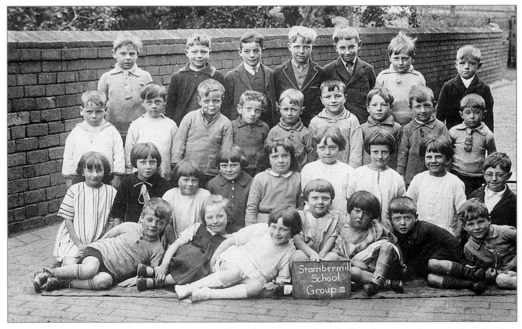

A Stambermill School group in the 1930s. The school was a church foundation and a mixed and infant school when it was built in 1852. It was enlarged in 1894. The building still exists but has now been converted to industrial use.

A boys' class at Orchard Lane, *c.* 1906. The boy marked with the cross was a member of the Kendrick family related by marriage to Mr Green, the Rating Officer, who lived in a large house behind the Congregational Church. Note the Eton collars of the pupils and also the two monitors or pupil teachers on the right.

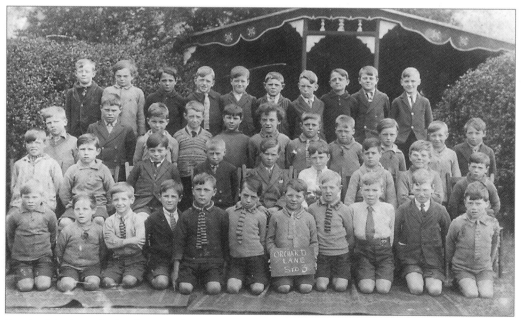

Standard 3 class, Orchard Lane School, *c.* 1929. The pavilion in the background often formed the backdrop for school groups and was situated between Orchard Lane and Valley Road schools. It belonged to a privately owned bowling club.

Standard 6 class, Orchard Lane School, *c.* 1929. It comprised thirty-nine pupils in the boys' department, aged between twelve and thirteen. Standards 5 and 6 were taught by two women teachers, the Misses Case and Morgan, who were strict disciplinarians.

Class 2, Orchard Lane School, *c.* 1929. This is a girls' department group of thirty-eight pupils. The photograph is again taken with the bowling club pavilion in the background.

Teachers from Orchard Lane School, *c.* 1910. Here are the female staff gathered around Miss Emma Pearson, head of the girls' department. She held that position for thirty-eight years. The young lady in the middle of the back row, Miss Annie Green, appears in the next photograph, still on the staff many years later. Note the exquisite dresses and elaborate hairdos.

Orchard Lane teachers in the 1940s. These were the teachers of Orchard Lane Junior Mixed School. Back row, left to right: Miss Morgan (later Mrs Green), Miss Chance (later Mrs Blackwell), Miss Annie Green, Mrs Simmonds. Front row: Miss Jones, Miss Davies (headmistress) and Miss Aston.

The cast of *Hiawatha*, performed in 1929. These eighteen braves and one squaw (male) were the cast in an Orchard Lane School concert staged in the Congregational School hall to raise funds for a new piano.

Valley Road Senior School, Year 1c, *c.* 1929. The familiar pavilion is in the background. Mr Harper, the headmaster, is seated on the left. The school was opened in 1911 and owed much to the pressures brought to bear on the county council by Mr Wrigley, the Unitarian minister. The older pupils from Orchard Lane were transferred here. Note that the class is mixed.

Valley Road School football team, 1948. Note the air raid shelter in the background. Back row, left to right: Mr Pearson, the sports master, M. Holloway, B. Hart, R. Powell, R. Perks, D. Bills, G. Stanier, B. Chell. Front row: E. Jenkins, C. Jordan, H. Scott, S. Schofield, F. Knowles, D. Little.

Valley Road cricket team, 1948. Back row, left to right: Mr Pearson, P. Drew, D. Bridgewater, A. Bradley, C. Hoppitt, Mr Harper (headmaster), C. Allport; Front row: D. Skidmore, F. Knowles, J. Price, E. Jenkins, B Cartwright, B. Dunn.

Valley Road School tug of war, *c.* 1948. The backdrop is Messrs Eveson Brothers' factory, the curved roof (Belfast) being widely used for Lye industrial buildings. Mr Pearson is again seeing fair play.

Wollescote infants' group, 1928. Crabbe Street School, Wollescote, was a contemporary of Orchard Lane. It closed in 1974, but its infants' department, opened in 1897, is still in use and is now known as Drummond Road School.

Cemetery Road School. This was an infants-only school, which opened in 1882, but it was always known as 'the little school'. It closed several years ago, but its premises remain standing.

Mr Bromley, the 'School Bobby'. During the interwar years truancy was firmly nipped in the bud by the School Attendance Officer. Mr Bromley served in that capacity for seventeen years. He was a familiar figure with his paperwork tucked under the stump of his right arm, a result of injuries sustained in the First World War; he learned to write with his left hand. He also lost part of his foot. Here he is shown as a happy family man.

Tiny tots at Lye Carnival, 1928. Young schoolchildren are being shepherded along Hay Green to the sports ground by Miss Kennard, later Mrs Skelding, a much loved teacher at Orchard Lane Infants' School for many years.

Fancy dress characters at Lye Carnival, 1928. These young people are assembled in the playground of Orchard Lane School, probably waiting to join the procession to the sports ground on Stourbridge Road. Valley Road School is visible behind the wall.

INDUSTRY

Thomas Perrins' proof house in the 1940s. At this time Sir Sidney Law JP owned the chain works founded in 1770 at Careless Green. This photograph shows the bed of the hydraulic device, left, with windlass, which could test chain strength to breaking point. The two men in the left foreground are inspecting railway couplings. Flaws capable of being repaired were dealt with by the two men at the hearth on the right. Howard Cooper at the far end of the gangway was well known for his work with the St John's Ambulance Brigade.

Oldnall colliery, *c.* 1907/8. Mobberley and Perry, brick manufacturers on The Hayes, took over Oldnall in about 1904 after it had lain unworked for twenty-five years. The man in the bowler hat was Caleb Thompson who had previously worked at Whitley Pit; he was Oldnall's manager. The young boy on the front row was Bob Brettell. An inclined plane ran from the pit to Hayes Wharf, 500 yards away. The Oldnall chimney was a landmark visible for miles. The pit finally closed in the early 1940s.

The factory of Hayes Tubes. Tube manufacture has been carried out here since the early 1930s but the buildings are older; they were where the hollow-ware trade of Lye began in 1863. They featured in Annie S. Swan's novel *A Bitter Debt* as Kingdom Bucket Works.

John Perks' factory, Church Street, 1960s. This was founded in 1861 as a nail-making concern and later, apart from smithing and drop forging, it manufactured vehicle springs, at first for horse-drawn vehicles, then for the motor industry.

The former Attwood works, The Hayes. This is one of the oldest industrial sites in Lye, originally the vice and anvil forge of Joseph Attwood, a relative of the Birmingham banking and Chartist family. It featured in the doggerel, *The Beauties of the Lye Waste*.

A backyard nail shop, *c*. 1900. A once common sight, this industry was especially associated with the mud houses on the Waste. However, mechanization killed the trade in the mid-nineteenth century; the living had always been uncertain with foggers (unscrupulous nailmasters) exploiting the workers. Note the older woman's 'hurden' apron — made of rough sacking or linen — and the small boy, wearing his Eton collar, peeping shyly round the door.

Baker's factory, King Street, was established on 10 June 1887 by Benjamin Baker who made nails. Forbidden by covenant to establish a factory in a residential area he made the building resemble a row of houses. In this way it put industrial spies off the scent and if he fell on hard times he could sell them as homes. In 1889 Baker began to make frost cogs and, by 1900, horseshoes. It was horseshoes, especially developed for the American market, which saved the firm in the 1960s. It moved to new premises on The Hayes in 1993.

ALL PREVIOUS LISTS CANCELLED.

The Lye Co-operative Society, Limited

LYE, NEAR STOURBRIDGE.

ESTABLISHED 1861,

—— JOHN PEARSON, Secretary. ——

GENERAL LIST (JUNE, 1888) OF

HAND-MADE HORSE NAILS

(C) BRAND, POINTED AND ORDINARY.

TEMPERED STEEL FROST NAILS

FROST SCREWS,

AND

SELF-FASTENING FROST STUDS.

Files, Rasps, Anvils, Vices, Bellows, Taps & Dies, Wheelwrights', Coach Builders', and Boat Builders' Ironwork; Backbands, Traces, Cable and Rigging Chains, Shackles, &c., Best Countersunk Clout Nails, Skip Nails, Basket and Hamper Fittings of all kinds, &c., &c.

Goods to the amount of £3 sent Carriage Paid to any Station in England, Ireland, Scotland, or Wales.

Cheques or Post Office Orders may be made payable to either the Society or the Secretary. The latter to be payable at the Lye Post Office.

These Prices are for Cash with Order, or satisfactory references, and are subject to alteration without notice.

Terms, ... *Monthly, or Nett on Journey.*

J. T. FORD, ENGRAVER & PRINTER, STOURBRIDGE.

An advertisement for Lye Co-operative Society, 1888. This was an unusual branch of the movement and was established in 1861, specializing in ironmongery and industrial goods. It ceased trading through poor, though not dishonest, money management.

Bert Bloomer at work in the 1960s. He is busy at the 'Oliver' at Benjamin Baker's, King Street. The Oliver was a treadle operated hammer, often blacksmith-made, and used extensively in the area for a variety of trades, including nail and chain making and hollow-ware manufacture.

Smith and anvil, a scene once familiar in Lye, particularly as the town was the centre of the anvil-making trade. Note the setts in front of the hearth.

A well bucket. This was typical of the wide range of products once made in the hollow-ware factories of Lye. Whereas the ordinary bucket would float on being lowered into the water this design allowed the bucket to sink mouth downwards and right itself during filling.

A galvanizer. After manufacture each individual item of hollow-ware was dipped in a pot of molten zinc (spelter) which made it rustproof. Here Bill Willetts, a life-long employee of Sargeant Turner, is galvanizing a dustbin.

The workforce of Albert Wilson and Sons, stampers and kitchenware manufacturers in Chapel Street in the 1890s. The frying pans held by the workman on the left were made to suspend on a hook over the open fire. They were stamped using a simple steam hammer.

J.P. Round's workforce, October 1922. The factory in Orchard Lane was established in 1849 for the manufacture of nails, chains and vices but in 1874 it began making hollow-ware goods. The man second from the right on the third row is presumably the 'gaffer' or foreman as he sports a bowler hat.

A Lye brickyard, *c.* 1920. There were many brickyards in Lye including Rufford, Timmis, Hickman and Hunt in Stambermill, Hadcroft across in New Farm, Harper-Moore in Park Road, Mobberley and Perry on The Hayes and G.K. Harrison in Dudley Road. By tradition women had always been employed in the brickyards, dancing on the local clay in bare feet to soften it up; as moulders they were expected to produce 1,025 bricks per day.

The workforce of Meshak Lavender. The firm established by Meshak Lavender in 1856 made high quality garments in its premises on the High Street. In 1900 his two sons ran separate businesses next door to each other. His grandson, Albert Lavender, is the young man standing on the right in the foreground of this picture.

H.T. Hazelwood, frost cog manufacturer. He established his workshop in Crabbe Street in 1882. Here he is shown with his son Clement, home from the Front during the First World War. Minnie the pony was a great character loved by all the family.

Henry Wooldridge and sons. Mr Wooldridge was a self-made man with a substantial factory in Bromley Street manufacturing horse shoes and frost cogs. The latter he invented in about 1880. Here he is shown in the 1870s with sons Sydney (born 1869) and Ernest (born 1860). Sydney became captain of Stourbridge Cycling Club and was a well-known writer on cycling matters. His father was also a bicycle enthusiast and an avid collector of curios.

LEISURE

Mr Cedric Hardwicke crowning the Lye Carnival Queen in 1930. He chose and crowned Gladys Price. This shows her coronation with her attendants, from left to right, Blanche Fletcher, Olive Griffiths, Irene Wassell and Elsie Westwood. The pages are Claude Cook and Joseph Beasley. Mrs Hardwicke is second from right.

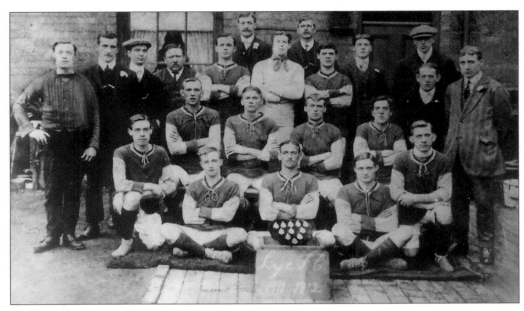

Lye Football Club, 1911/12. Back row, left to right: Mr Hill (trainer), H. Share, F. Haddock, L. Newey, J. Davis, A. Pritchard (secretary), ? Barnbrook, W. Trevis, ? Price, ? Davis. The players are, third row: ? Willetts, G. Trevis, J. Brettell. Second row: J. Pearson (captain), S. Hingley, S. Pearson, G. Pearson. Front row: ? Bashford, ? Keightly, ? Morgan, ? Freeman, ? Pritchard.

Wollescote Villa football team. They were the winners of the Brooks Cup and Alhambra Cup and medals in 1913-14. Like the previous shot this was taken outside the Castle public house in Balds Lane.

Lye Unitarians Football Club, 1920-1. They were the finalists and league winners of Lye and District Sunday School League. Players include Parkes, Pritchard, Brettell, Porter, A. Pardoe, Hipkiss, Westwood, T. Pardoe, Parish and Rumsey.

Lye Cricket Club, 1897. The club challenged and defeated a team of twenty Lye businessmen as a celebration of Queen Victoria's Diamond Jubilee on 22 June 1897. The batsman standing on the extreme right only had one arm. At his right shoulder is Samuel Bridge, headmaster of Orchard Lane School. Note the variety of headgear.

Lye Cricket Club, 2nd Eleven, 1924. These were the Kidderminster League winners. Back row, left to right: Tom Skelding, Wilf Parkes, Sid Holloway, Bill Trevis, Stan Wooldridge, Harold Robinson, Bill Boucher, Joe Huband. Seated: Harry Bache, Dick Rhodes, George Cook, Bob Brettell, Sam Pardoe, Len Wakeman.

Timmis's Cricket Club, 1920s. This team reputedly had the honour of making the longest hit in cricketing history. Their ground was near the railway line and once a ball was knocked on to a moving coal wagon which finished its journey at Worcester.

An early photograph of Lye Bowling Club. The green was in the vicinity of Hill Road. Members are all smartly dressed suggesting it was an élite club. Note the variety of headgear and jackets.

The Lye Liberals bowling team in the 1950s. Back row, left to right: R. Hudson, A. Cartwright, L. Pardoe (cartoonist and creator of 'Chipper' in the *Evening Dispatch*), A. Wiley, R. Pearson. Middle row: J. Robinson, A. Homer, B. Pearson, F. Fairman, P. Clewes, L. Turner, J. Cook, A. Hall, H. Cooper. Front row: H. Hart, A. Hingley, R. Turner, J. Williams, Mr Entwistle (of the Temp), E. Homer (his projectionist), D. Turner, L. Turner, T. Hadlington.

W. Smith and Monty, *c.* 1930. Mr Smith of Attwood Street was a well-known character. He bred fighting cocks and bull terriers for illegal contests, continuing a long tradition of barbaric sports. Lye has the unenviable reputation of being the last place in England to practise bull-baiting (on the Cross). Monty has a wonderful expression.

The cast of *Princess Ju-Ju*, an operetta written and produced by Mrs H.C. Darby in 1914 and staged by the Congregationalists in the Vic and Temp. About to be beheaded is Claude Aston; the Lord High Executioner is Miss Lilian Westwood.

The Victoria cinema, or more commonly the Vic, was built in just two weeks in 1913, mainly from corrugated iron with a Belfast roof, a popular pattern in Lye. Designed by a Lye-born man, Mr Hugh Folkes, the theatre served the area for fifty years and alternated between films, live theatre, skating and wrestling.

A queue at the Temp. This is a late 1920s shot of an eager crowd outside the Temperance Hall built in 1874, but later used as a cinema. It was run by Mr Entwistle, owner of the Danic, a grocery shop in the High Street, and also an urban district councillor. He ran it more as a social service than for profit. Educational films were often shown free to local schools.

The opening of Lye Park in 1932. Mr Ernest Stevens, local industrialist and benefactor, is sitting outside Wollescote Hall on the occasion of his handing over house and grounds to the UDC as a public park. Rufus Dunn, chairman of the UDC, is on his right with F. Evans to his left. A young Wesley Perrins stands behind him to the right, flanked by G. Eveson on his right and H. Barlow on his left.

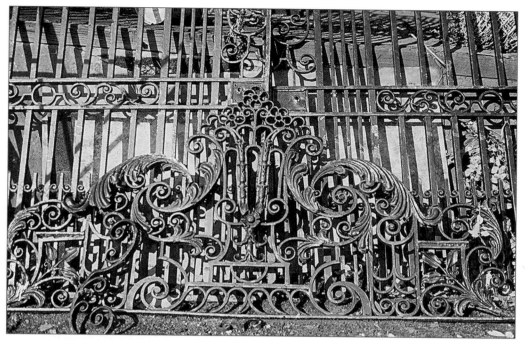

The main gates at Stevens Park. This picture shows details of the exquisite workmanship of the main gates to the park. They were apparently sold as scrap to a local metal broker by the council during the war. Their fate remains a mystery.

The original bottom entrance to Stevens Park. This stood at Ludgebridge Brook in the days when the park was completely fenced in and had full-time keepers to supervise the grounds, which boasted gardens, a bandstand, bowling greens and tennis courts.

The Coronation committee of 1911. Major Pardoe, headmaster of Crabbe Street School, sits fifth from the left. To facilitate the organization of the celebrations he was allowed to close the school for a week. Note the enormous hats sported by the lady committee members.

A Coronation group in Fletcher Street, 1953. Like most towns in the country Lye had many street parties to celebrate this event. Considering that this photograph was taken on a June day everyone is well wrapped up and the sky looks ominous, but nothing can wipe the smiles from their faces.

Hickman Street belles, 1953. Three little girls pose outside a house decorated for the Coronation. They had all made a special effort with their outfits and headgear.

Happy playmates in Union Passage. This 1950s photograph shows a group of little friends with a once-popular children's toy, the scooter. Note the nail shop with its shutters closed in the background.

A Lye group at Weston Hall, *c.* 1967. Lye and Wollescote Allotment and Gardens Association are enjoying their annual outing. Featured are, back row, left to right: Len Wood, Lottie Wood, Fred Whitehouse, Bill Willetts (secretary), Frank Dickens, George Albert Cook. Middle row: Mrs Jones, -?-, Mildred Dickens. Front row: Harry Jones, Vera Willetts, Joe Willetts (treasurer), Mrs Whitehouse, Mrs P. Share, Mrs Dickens. Peter Guest is the young boy in the foreground.

A chapel outing, *c.* 1957. This happy snapshot shows a group from Salem Chapel in Pedmore Road on a visit to Trentham Gardens in Staffordshire.

Private Harry Head, St John's Ambulance Brigade, August 1920. This photograph shows him when the Lye Corps won the District and Dudley Challenge Shield. The remainder of the team were Corporal B. Skelding, Corporal H. Cooper and Privates Taylor and Stinton.

1st Lye Company, Boys' Brigade, c. 1935. Back row, left to right: R. Collins, J. Beasley, D. Brooks, P. Perks, E. Whiley. G. Kendrick. Third row: G. Cartwright, B. Homer, Revd Mr Taylor Richardson, J. Wood, K. Hamblett. Second row: S. Yeadon, L. Cooper, ? Scott, C. Little, D. Perry, J. Brettell. Front row: H. Stinton, A. Stinton, S. Hart, T. Bullingham, R. Perks.

Millers scouts, 1915. Some founder members of St Mark's scouts are shown here. Standing at the back, from left to right, are W. Gibbs, F. Davis, H. Weston, V. Skelding. Seated are E. Morris and Claude Aston. At the front are C. Hart, T. Bills and B. Morris.

Millers scouts, 1915. This is another early photograph of Stambermill scouts. Seated in the centre is C.J. Aston, later mayor of Stourbridge. On the extreme right is A.E. Morris, later Archbishop of Wales.

Prims scouts, Bewdley, 1928. The Primitive Methodist scouts are here demonstrating their athletic prowess at camp in Bewdley.

Prims scouts in the 1920s. All are very smartly turned out.

Prims scouts, 1953. This photograph shows three members of this Methodist troop. From left to right are G.S.M. Wilson, Queen's scout, Kelvin Hughes and S.M. Ralph Davies. Mr Wilson was a much admired and respected Scout Master for many years.

Congs guides, 1933. Back row, left to right: ? Bridgewater, ? Tonks (patrol leader), ? Chapman, A. Gordon, M. Tonks, W. Beasley (patrol leader), M. Pass, M. Whyley, B. Tonks, N. Taylor (patrol leader), E. Southall, I. Bullingham. Second row: I. Bubb, M. Bullingham, H. Chapman, D. Watkins, E. Morris, -?-, V. Tonks, H. Bromyard, V. Sidaway, W. Walters, C. Bridgewater. Third row: -?-, Mr Beddall (superintendent), Revd Mr Rees, Mrs Beddall (captain), Miss Goodman (commissioner), Miss Chattin (assistant commissioner), E. Whyley (lieutenant), N. Connop. Front row: -?- Pearson, J. Pearson, E. Wall, E. Cartwright, D. Heathcote, J. Chance, M. Poole, L. Beddall.

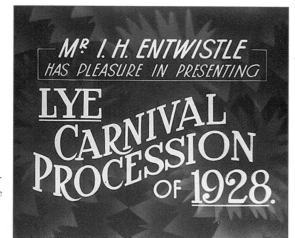

A film still from the film covering the Lye Carnival in 1928. It was held to raise funds for Corbett Hospital. Festivities lasted for a whole week and a film was made by Pathétone News of the schoolchildren's parade on Wednesday and the procession on the following Saturday.

St George at the Lye Carnival, 1928. The dragon, with its dozens of human feet, is making its way along the High Street watched by a large admiring crowd. St George is at the front on the left. A procession of decorated floats is following behind.

The Mount Tabor tableau at the carnival, 1928. 'Top Chapel' had a horse-drawn float in the carnival, entitled the 'League of Nations'. As well as entries from the churches themselves, most Sunday schools were also represented. The parade was over a mile long.

The carnival crowd at the Cross, 1928. This shot shows part of the mile-long procession wending its way towards the sports ground in Stourbridge Road, which had been opened that year. On the left is Harvey's barber's and tobacconist's shop. On the other side of the road is the ancient Lye Cross Inn. At the time the licensee was Polly Brooks who also owned the substantial fruit and vegetable wholesale/retail business a few doors away.

Another carnival crowd of 1928. Lye High Street has never been so crowded as on the Saturday of the carnival. The last float has passed and the crowd surge forward. On the right corner is the Midland Bank. The Birmingham-bound Midland Red bus at the back of the picture is marooned in a sea of bodies.

The Lye Carnival Queen of 1954. Chosen by Jack Downing, the Queen rides in splendour. She was Mrs Mary Hipkiss, née Cartwright, and had married just five days previously. The car was provided by J.P. Eveson and the dress by E. Allport. In the background to the right is the old National School, then used as a church hall, and on the left is the Clifton cinema.

A gathering at the RAOB Lily Lodge, 1950s. Members of the Royal Antediluvian Order of Buffaloes are photographed here in full regalia. Such lodges met in local public houses. Lily Lodge was founded in 1925. Note the buffalo horns overhead.

South Wales glee singers, 1926. Wesley Perrins, who could not claim to be a singer, is seated among members of a Welsh Miners' Choir touring the area during the 1926 General Strike. He is simply showing his solidarity with their cause.

PERSONALITIES

Denys Brooks, 1921–1997. A native of Stambermill, Denys trained as an engineer and for many years worked at Lamb Hingley. He had many interests, including bell-ringing and genealogy, but his overriding passion was local history. Though a very private person, he was well known and respected in Lye and he collected the bulk of the photographs for this book through this personal contact.

King George V decorating Lance-Corporal Thomas Bryan. Thomas was born in Bott Lane, Stambermill, on 21 January 1882, but the family later moved to the north. He was awarded the Victoria Cross for his outstanding gallantry in the First World War at Vimy Ridge on 9 April 1917. As a lance-corporal in the 25th Northumberland Fusiliers he knocked out a strongly defended German machine-gun post single-handed. Wounded in action three times, he returned to the Front each time on his recovery. He died in Bentley on 13 October 1945.

The last meeting of Lye and Wollescote Urban District Council, 1933. Around the table are, left to right, C.E. Wassell, Wesley Perrins, G.A. Rhodes (Housing Manager), W.S. Mobberley, Frank Evans (Vice-Chairman), Rufus Dunn (Chairman), H.E. Folkes (Surveyor), H. Barlow, G.H. Eveson, Edward Allport, J.A. Gauden. Standing are J. Basterfield (Mobberley's Clerk), E. Porter (Assistant to Mr Rhodes), Dr Darby, H. Poole (Sanitary Inspector), H. Bird (Rating Officer). The portrait is of Amos Perrins and the ornate chair was a gift from Mr Webster of Ye Olde Antique Shoppe.

Wesley Perrins was born in Balds Lane in 1905 and died in January 1990. He was a man of many parts, a staunch lifelong socialist, Trades Union official, urban district councillor, borough and county councillor and Member of Parliament. Locally, he was a popular Methodist local preacher, dinner and schoolroom speaker. He was an avid researcher of Lye history and wrote several books on the subject.

Joseph Westwood, MP, PC. He was born on 11 February 1884 on the Lye Waste, but the family moved to Scotland when he was still a boy. He was a miner, like his father, becoming industrial organizer for Fife minefields and later political organizer for Scottish miners. In 1922 he was elected Labour MP for Peebles. In 1935 he became MP for Stirling and Falkirk and in 1945, at the Labour landslide victory, he became Secretary of State for Scotland in Attlee's cabinet. He was tragically killed with his wife in a motoring accident in 1948.

Florence Pritchard, MBE. She was born in Vicarage Road in 1888, but later moved to Bewdley. In Bewdley she was involved in local government for over fifty years, becoming mayor in 1958 and 1959. At 98 she was the Midlands' oldest serving councillor and was 102 when she died.

Sir Michael Higgs was born in Hill Road in 1912. A local solicitor, he served as county councillor for Staffordshire and Worcestershire and was MP for Bromsgrove from 1950 to 1955. He received his knighthood in 1969.

Henry Wooldridge was born at Careless Green, Wollescote, on 14 February 1840, the son of a nail-maker. Self-educated, he worked hard to improve himself and by 1874 had a nail-making factory in Bromley Street, employing 100 men. As this trade was in decline he switched to manufacturing horseshoes, and he invented the frost cog in about 1880. He was also a great chess player and flautist. Note his horseshoe tie-pin.

Mr Ernest Stevens was a local hollow-ware
manufacturer and also a great benefactor to Lye
and other Black Country towns. It was he who
presented Lye and Wollescote Park to the
community in 1932 and one each to
Stourbridge and Quarry Bank. He also donated
Mary Stevens' Maternity Home to Stourbridge.

Wilfred Hill. Born on Lye Cross in 1869, son
of the Lye photographer Athelstan Hill,
Wilfred trained as a chemist and enjoyed a
distinguished career: he was the inventor of the
popular product, Brylcreem. Much involved in
politics, in 1913, as a Liberal candidate, he
(unsuccessfully) opposed Sir Austen
Chamberlain in the General Election for the
East Worcestershire constituency. A linguist
and poet, he was also a journalist on the
Birmingham Post, *Mail* and *Argus*.

Alfred Edwin Morris was born in 1894 in Stourbridge Road where his father had a jeweller's shop. He attended Stambermill School. Later he became Professor of Hebrew and Theology at Lampeter College and was also Mayor of Lampeter. Between 1945 and 1957 he was Bishop of Monmouth and in 1957 was created Archbishop of Wales, retiring in 1971.

Albert Pearson. After leaving Orchard Lane School at the age of twelve he worked for a Cradley Heath engineering company. When old enough he became a local preacher, and a Methodist minister in 1911. His ministry was mainly served in the Penzance area. On his death, when he was 102, he was the oldest Methodist minister in the country.

Reverend Alan Green was the son of the Lye rating officer. After a successful career as a journalist he entered the ministry of the Congregational Church in 1917. Eventually he became moderator of the London Province.

Reverend T.M.W. Clewes, MA. He was born in Bott Lane, Stambermill, in 1891. The son of a blacksmith, he had experienced an early call to the ministry. In 1915 he passed the entrance examination for Nottingham Congregational Institution. His training complete, he was intent on devoting himself to foreign mission work and served many years in India. On his return he continued to preach until into his nineties. He died on 30 May 1984.

Mr Albert Brooks with his wife and daughter. Born in Vicarage Road, he became chief assistant at Tividale Council School and Principal of Tividale Evening Institute before becoming head of Corby Council School when it opened in 1914. Under him the school became celebrated for its musical achievements. He was very active in Corby's public life, being a local councillor and JP.

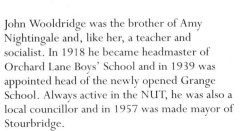

Amy Nightingale, née Wooldridge. She was born in Wollescote in 1879 becoming a teacher in 1897 and later headmistress of Swan Lane Infants' School, Evesham, where she started Worcestershire's first nursery school in 1925. She was Evesham's first woman councillor, alderman and mayor. She died in 1970 at the age of ninety.

John Wooldridge was the brother of Amy Nightingale and, like her, a teacher and socialist. In 1918 he became headmaster of Orchard Lane Boys' School and in 1939 was appointed head of the newly opened Grange School. Always active in the NUT, he was also a local councillor and in 1957 was made mayor of Stourbridge.

Major Pardoe. He was born in 1860 in Skeldings Lane and attended Lye Church School where he became a monitor at the age of ten. A pupil teacher at thirteen, he qualified in December 1881. In June 1882 he was appointed head of the new Crabbe Street School and remained there until he retired in 1925. He died in 1950, but is still remembered with much respect.

George Thomas lived in Stourbridge Road and attended Orchard Lane School, followed by Stourbridge Grammar School and St John's College, Cambridge, where he read Classics. During the Second World War he was an army captain. Later he became Principal of Dunstable College, Herts.

Harry Hill (1891–1991). Lye's first librarian, he enjoyed only an elementary schooling, but through his involvement with the WEA educated himself. He had always been an avid bookworm and was appointed part-time librarian in a room at Alton House. When the new library opened on the site in 1935 he became full-time branch librarian. He was a phenomenal walker and lived to be 100.

Henry Hill, born on Waste Bank in 1849, was educated at Lye Church School, becoming a pupil teacher there. He later qualified at Cheltenham Training College. In 1873 he emigrated to Canterbury, New Zealand, teaching on South Island. In 1877 he was appointed Inspector of Schools for the Hawkes Bay district of North Island, retiring in 1914. He died in 1933. He was an expert on volcanoes and Maori culture.

Fred Allen. Born in 1891 into a chain-making family, he was himself a chain-maker for the whole of his working life. He was President of the Chain-makers' Association for twenty-four years. A qualified tutor, he also taught shorthand for fifty-five years after working all day in the forge. He was a member of Lye Congregational Church choir as well as other choirs and choral societies.

Sir Cedric Hardwicke, the son of a local doctor, was born in 1893 at Lye Cross House. He made his public acting debut at Stambermill Church School in 1900. He graduated from local stage shows to Birmingham Rep. and thence via London theatres to Hollywood where he became an internationally famous film star. He died in 1964.

Noel Brettell was a member of a well-known Lye family. He was born in the High Street in 1908. Educated at Orchard Lane School, Stourbridge Grammar School and Birmingham University, he moved to Rhodesia in 1930. There he was involved in teaching for thirty years. He became a national figure in Zimbabwe through his writings, particularly his poetry. He died on 29 November 1991.

Bill Pardoe was born on 18 September 1904 in a house in Lye High Street where his father had a photography business. He was himself a talented photographer and also an expert artist in stained glass. Witley Court, former home of the Earls of Dudley, was his great love. He lived in the grounds in his later years and produced a book on its days of glory. He died in Scotland in September 1991. He has left a wonderful legacy of local views of Lye, some reproduced in this book, courtesy of John Cooksey.

William Hart, like Bill Pardoe, is a talented photographer. Born in Bromley Street, he opened a photography shop in the High Street in 1958 and specialized in portraits, winning many international awards. He too has recorded Lye prior to and since its redevelopment. Some photographs are reproduced in this book and a collection of his commercial postcards of the town are available in the shop.

Annie S. Swan was born in Scotland in 1859. Her husband, Dr Burnett-Smith, was assistant to Dr Hardwicke for six months in 1893. While Annie described Lye as 'an appalling place to live in', she used it as the setting for her best-selling novel *A Bitter Debt: A Tale of the Black Country.* She died in 1943.

POSTSCRIPT

A view of the High Street in Edwardian days. To the top right are the fine Rhodes buildings, built by local brick manufacturer and public figure, Thomas Rhodes. They incorporated many different types of bricks with 'moral' plaques on the upper storey, 'Be not slothful' and 'Diligent in business'. Note the cobbled street, tram lines and poles.

A turn-of-the-century postcard of Lye High Street on the Waste. This area was known as Lye Village and the Unitarian Church on the left as the Village Church. Note the cobbled street, tram poles and lines, the wagon on the left and the number of dogs and fly-posters.

The Dock. This ran parallel to the High Street in the 'village' area. Note the entrance to Jeavons' bungalow bath works. The bricks in the buildings and walls would have been made locally but little attention has been paid to their laying.

An undated view of Lye station in the days of steam. The lamppost, child's apron and the ladies' tam-o'-shanters on the left suggest an early 1900s date. Note the large number of station staff on the right.

Ludgebridge Brook, Lye. This is a view before the 'Spout' council houses were built but after the park had been acquired, suggesting an early 1930s date. By this time Perrins Lane (left) and Brook Holloway (right) had been developed.

ACKNOWLEDGEMENTS

Special thanks to M. Ayres, G. Beckley, A. Brooks, J. Cooksey, R. Cooper, F. Guest, S. Hill, F. Lowe, Stourbridge Police and Coroner's Office. Also to S. Allen, Baker Horseshoes, P. Bedford, H. & L. Bromley, J.H. Brettell, R. Brettell, G. Burrows, Coseley Archives, *County Express and Stourbridge News*, B. de Havilland, R. Fieldhouse, J. Firth, A. Fox, M. Foxall, R. Frogatt, Fusiliers Museum, Northumberland, C. Gadd, W. Gibbs, Revd A. Green, J. Green, M. Hale, C. Harper, D. Harrison, W. Hart, M. Heathcote, Lady Higgs, G. Hill, Mr & Mrs Hipkiss, E. Hodges, W. Jay-Ingley, M. Jones, Mr Kitson, A. Lavender, B. Lowe, Lye Library, T. Merrick, National Maritime Museum, E. Pardoe, E. Pearson, J. Phillips, Mr Rowley, Salvation Army, I. Smith, F. Spittle, Stirling Library, Stourbridge Library, F. Tristram, A. Turnbull Library, Wellington, New Zealand, W. Whitworth, Mrs Woodall, Revd D. Woodhouse and G. Wooldridge.

Many of these photographs, plus correspondence, were retrieved hastily from Denys Brooks' house immediately after his death. Every effort has been made to trace those people who sent them to him and Pat Dunn apologizes to anyone who has not been mentioned above.

An early view of Perrins Lane. It shows what appears to be a substantial house, right, and a cottage with nail shop, left. No development has taken place on the opposite side of the road.

BRITAIN IN OLD PHOTOGRAPHS

To order any of these titles please telephone our distributor, Littlehampton Book Services on 01903 721596

For a catalogue of these and our other titles please ring Regina Schinner on 01453 731114